# CAREGIVING FROM YOUR SPIRITUAL STRENGTHS

How to Create a Healing
Environment for Your
Care Receiver *and for You!*

## THE 10 FUNDAMENTAL
## PRINCIPLES FOR OPTIMAL SUCCESS

## The Spiritual Strengths Healing Plan

Richard P. Johnson, Ph.D.

ISBN  978-0-9895130-5-0

10  9  8  7  6  5  4  3  2  1

First Edition

*Cover design by Megan Irwin*

*Edited by Maggie Singleton*

Printed in the United States of America

# BOOKS IN THE SPIRITUAL STRENGTHS HEALING SERIES

## by Richard P. Johnson

- God Give Me Strength! Finding the Inner Power to Turn Your Illness/Brokenness/Life Transition Around

- Discover Your Spiritual Strengths: Find Health, Healing, and Happiness (flagship book of the Spiritual Strengths Healing Plan)

- Body, Mind, Spirit: Tapping the Healing Power Within

- Prayers for Spiritual Strength: Physical Illnesses, Emotional Broken Places, and/or Spiritual Dis-eases

- The Ten Most Effective Self-Care Healing Techniques: What You Can Do to Maximize Your Healing Journey

- The Power of Smiling: Using Positive Psychology for Optimal Health & Healing

- Healing Wisdom: 101 Spiritual Truths for Healing Your Illness

- Healing and Depression: Finding Peace in the Midst of Transition, Turmoil, or Illness

- Staying Spiritually Centered for Optimal Healing: Even When You're Sick or Life Seems Out of Control

- Seeking Significance: How to Discover New Self-Direction and New Life-Purpose Beyond Your (Unwanted) Life Transition

**Caregiving Titles**

- Caregiving from Your Spiritual Strengths: The Ten Fundamental Principles for Optimal Success

- Because I Care...Inspiration for Caregiving for Spouses, Health Care Personnel, Family & Friends

# The Spiritual Strengths Healing Plan

The Spiritual Strengths Healing Plan allows you to harness your internal healing power! It is not "faith healing" in which one relies on divine intervention as the sole means for physical cure, nor does it promise cure. Its purpose is healing and is best seen as a supplement to and support for current medical practices. The Spiritual Strengths Healing Plan's philosophy holds that each individual needs to seek the best and most appropriate medical and psychological care they can, in accord with their own personal wishes, and supplement their care with this Plan.

Please note that you will see the word "illness" throughout this book in its broadest sense and may indicate any (or a combination) of the following:

## I. Physical Sicknesses

Cancer, heart disease, MS, Lupus, migraine, addictions, hypochondriasis, pain, weight management/loss, smoking cessation, pneumonia, COPD, hypertension, arthritis, immune disorders, Parkinson's, diabetes, stroke, chronic fatigue etc., etc.

## II. Psychological Issues

Anxiety, depression, personality disorders, OCD, manipulation, stress, bi-polar disorder, etc., etc.

### III. Emotional Issues

Being unrealistic, lacking responsibility, low-self-esteem, career focus issues, poor organization skills, family disharmony, anger management, fears, perfectionism, marriage discontent, lifelessness, infidelity, irritability, chronic lateness, caregiving, etc., etc.

### IV. Spiritual Dis-eases

Peace of mind and heart, un-forgiveness, existential angst, inner pain, grudges, scrupulosity, incomplete developmental transitions, guilt, grief and unresolved grief, regrets, blame, disappointments, so-called "unfinished business," resentments, etc., etc.

### V. Spiritual Direction & Growth

Gaining better clarity of God's plan in your life, and breaking through barriers that may be hindering your faith journey.

## *Where do you need healing?*

*For more information about the Spiritual Strengths Healing Plan, log on to...*

*www.SpiritualStrengthsHealing.com*

# The Spiritual Strengths Healing Institute

*Learning the art of healing for self and others*

# Contents

# Introduction

This is the sixth book I've written on caregiving and the second one in this series. This book is a compilation of all of the many years of investigating, researching, and teaching I've had the honor to carry out while serving caregivers. But more than that, this book is a distillation of what I have heard directly from caregivers in private counseling sessions and from innumerable hours facilitating literally dozens of caregiver support groups. From among all these experiences, I've gleaned ten principles that I believe capture the heart and soul of the caregiving call. These ten are the necessary and sufficient conditions for success in caregiving...embrace these ten, learn them, and practice them and you will not only be doing all you can for your care receiver, you will be elevating the caregiving role into a personal vocation of immense and long-lasting value for you.

I've been privileged to hear and re-hear caregiver stories, their joys and their laments, their successes and failures, and their hopes and their sadness. I've sat by bedsides while the physician delivered the terrible news of the diagnosis. And right there with me stood the spouse (or adult child, sister or brother, other family member, or friend)—now shaking—who had no real idea that they had just been enlisted into the ranks of *caregiving* with no preparation, training, or support at all. They felt alone, scared, and emotionally overwhelmed.

This book is built on the central conviction that caregiving can be one of the most instructive endeavors that you can ever enter; it presents you with a curriculum of personal growth and development unlike any other. Caregiving is sometimes stern, frequently frustrating, occasionally overwhelming, consistently demanding, and always challenging. Yet, on the other hand, caregiving brings many gifts: you will never learn patience like you will in the caregiving role, or kindness, or compassion, or peace, or wisdom, or simplicity, or courage like caregiving can teach it. When you cooperate with caregiving, when you flow with caregiving, it can shape you into the true "you" that you have always wanted to be. If, on the other hand, you resist or fight against caregiving, it can wear you down and even wear you out.

I have so much empathy for caregivers—these armies of people pressed into service in the sometimes messy and always taxing trenches of caregiving with little or no warning and even less assistance. They had no idea that they were forfeiting so much at that very moment, that their lives would never be the same again, nor that they would be forced to not only confront illness, but also forced to face themselves in ways both challenging and demanding they've not dreamed of before. This book is dedicated to all those who give care to persons with illness or other issues. These devoted folks, regardless of where and how they serve, are truly the unsung soldiers and heroes of the illness wars.

I wrote this book for any person who is or anticipates being called upon to care for someone with illness. This includes—

- Spouses, family members (caring for a family member presents some special challenges), and friends.

- In-home caregivers (volunteer or paid) from agencies, churches, community organizations, and the like.

- The many different caregivers in the medical setting...RNs, LPNs, nursing assistants, and all the many other professionals who regularly give care to persons with illness.

While each of these roles is different, they all have the same thread of heart care that is quite similar. I've learned that the caregiving principles that undergird the work of all caregivers, regardless of the setting where they serve, are almost identical. I've boiled these principles down from an array of many into a manageable list of ten...the ten fundamental principles of caregiving. But I hope to give you more than a recitation of principles that alone can sound bland and somewhat academic. What I've tried to do is also give you effective caregiving practices that naturally flow from these ten fundamental principles. It's in the practices, not the principles, where we find the heartbeat of true caregiving and the "meat" that can spell the difference between you finding the caregiving journey fulfilling, or one that will eventually "do you in."

Illness is daunting, and caring for a person suffering with illness can be equally daunting—but in different ways. Caregivers feel pain, but it is pain of a different sort than what *care receivers* feel. Caregivers move through successive stages just as their care receiver moves through them. There is a symbiotic relationship between caregiver and care receiver—as one "moves," so does the other; as one's energy, and stamina, and perseverance ebbs and flows, so does the other. How one is feeling dramatically affects the other.

The relationship between the caregiver and the care receiver is at the core of this book. The relationship is almost sacred in that its quality determines so much of what will or will not emerge in the healing process. This relationship brings challenges at every turn; and the caregiver needs three things to successfully meet these challenges: 1) information, 2) support, and 3) a new perspective that the caregiving role has much to teach. It's my hope that this book offers you some answers to these three essentials of caregiving.

Grateful for your continuing care,

*Richard P. Johnson*

# Caregiving Principle One

## Your Unique Personality, Animated by Your Spiritual Strengths, is Your Most Important Caregiving Tool

Everyone has a personality...yet, why do we have one; what is our personality for...what is its function? Certainly there is no other personality like yours. There isn't another one like yours on the whole face of the earth; there never has been; and there never will be—you are the absolutely special rendition of God's grace compacted into the very small space of your personality.

There is only one reason you have a personality and that is to express the special combination of God's grace in you. Your personality achieves the goal of self-expression by performing the following six functions:

- Believing
- Perceiving
- Thinking
- Feeling
- Deciding
- Acting

All six of these functions are simultaneously and constantly operating without your conscious awareness. No one in the whole world behaves like you do...no one perceives or thinks or feels or decides or acts quite like you either—you are an exceptional, unparalleled, and notable individual just the way you are. I've described these six functions in the book <u>Discover Your Spiritual Strengths</u>, which is the "flagship" book of the Spiritual Strengths Healing Plan series of books. I invite you to look through this book, if you haven't already, to get as firm a grasp of these six personality functions as you can. Doing this will not only give you a much deeper understanding of how your personality operates, it will also offer a keener insight into your illness care receiver.

You have been gifted, as has everyone, with extraordinary gifts that give energy to your personality so you can be the fullness of your giftedness to the world. These gifts, or what I prefer to call spiritual strengths, give you the distinctiveness that is you—the matchless amalgam of grace and power and light that you are called to use to illuminate the world. You are at your best and holiest when you're "in" your spiritual strengths. Your spiritual strengths define you in the universe of God; your spiritual strengths couldn't be more personally important.

Each of your six personality functions has one premier gift or spiritual strength that serves as the power for that function so you can keep going. The power you require to operate your personality isn't material; it's not tangible—this magnificent power comes only from God. No one knows why you were given the spiritual strengths that you have. They are pure gift, and they propel you to be all that you can be.

Your personality is the internal mechanism that determines how and in what frame of mind you do virtually everything in your life. It's your personality that generates that urge to eat that piece of chocolate cake, and it's also your personality that can lead you to overcome the urge and pass it up. It's your personality that makes you sling that stinging accusation at your spouse, or friend, or co-worker, neighbor, or anyone…just as it's your personality that moves you to apologize for it afterward.

Actually it's not your personality per se but the way you choose to use your personality that determines how you use the six functions of your personality. So, it's the way you use this marvelous tool of your personality that determines how you will perform this new (or old) role of caregiving. Just as important, it's how you use your personality that creates how you feel as you move through the labyrinthine challenges that caregiving presents to you.

## Carol's Lament

Carol opened the front door to her mother's house as she had done every day since her mother was diagnosed with bowel cancer. Her mother, now receiving outpatient radiation treatment, didn't answer Carol when she greeted her mother. Her mother's sad, sullen, and morose expression twisted Carol's emotions into a knot of defiance. Her mom's 'You have to take care of me' attitude added a few more twists. But it was when Carol's mom asked her 'where she had been last evening that she didn't call' that Carol couldn't contain her emotions any longer and blurted out, *"Ma, you know I have a life to live, too. I have a family, and a full-time job, and all the responsibility that goes with all that. I try to do all I can for you, but you don't seem to understand or care about how all of this affects me…you only see things from your side."*

With that, Carol turned away from her mother and with tears streaming down her face, jumped into her car and took off. In half an hour, Carol was back with her mom, but she left her normal buoyant demeanor behind and in a blank silence went about the tasks of attending to her mother's needs.

Such toxic and painful caregiver encounters are common. They are the consequence of many beliefs left unrecognized, blurred perceptions, unclarified thoughts, feelings left unfocused, decisions made in haste, and behaviors misinterpreted. In short, such regrettable incidents as these (and many more) are the consequence of an unexamined personality...a personality that wants to do what is "right," but becomes shell-shocked, numb, and ever-traumatized mostly because the caregiver is unaware of how to use her personality in the face of the unrelenting pressure of illness. Your personality is a tool, and a very effective one, if and when it is sharpened, oiled, and used with precision. How is this accomplished in caregiving?

### *Get to Know Your Personality Very Well*

Many people ask me how they can better use their spiritual strengths while offering care. My answer is always the same: get to know your own personality better. This is the best advice I can offer from the thousands of caregivers I've encountered. The better you know your personality, the more aware you become of the way your personality operates and the more you can come to realize the benefits of *caregiving* and let go of what can hamper you. As you come to see more clearly how you may be misusing your personality (by ignoring your beliefs, attitudes, and values; turning a blind eye to new insights; blocking creative thinking; remaining out of "touch" with your feelings; refusing to consider new choices; and inhibiting invigorating actions), you will quite naturally elevate your caregiving and indeed your entire life to new heights of satisfaction, fulfillment, and even pleasure.

If Carol had developed a keener awareness of her personality, she would not have experienced the embarrassing and guilt-producing incident with her mom. Personality awareness isn't something that happens by itself in a flash of insight, rather it's a day-to-day monitoring of how the six functions of your personality move in an internal dance flowing one to another.

Most of the time, we're quite unaware of how our personality is moving us. We are frequently blind to the forces that trigger our personality functions to flow one way rather than another and how these forces permeate our being. Left unattended, your personality will begin to control you rather than you controlling (or using) it to serve your needs and desires. Caregiving requires that you come to know the unique strengths that power and propel your personality, as well as the shadows and compulsions that may inhibit it. Without this awareness, you are left to drift aimlessly on an uncharted ocean—feeling tense, anxious, and uncertain.

The big question of personality is who (or what) is in charge; who is running your personality "show?" Who is performing the executive competencies of your personality? This book is designed to help you gain control of your personality. You will learn how to gain command of yourself rather than unknowingly giving that command over to other forces, persons, etc.

### Your Six Personality Strengths

You can identify your six spiritual strengths by taking the Spiritual Strengths Healing Profile (SSHP). The SSHP asks you to respond to 120 statements on a scale of 1 to 10. While the statements are penetrating, they are not hard. You do not need to study before taking the SSHP...it's totally a subjective opinion profile, so there is no right or wrong answers. The SSHP clearly tells you your most powerful spiritual strengths in each of your six personality functions. These six words together make up your spiritual personality "fingerprint"—an identity that no one else can claim but you. Go to www.spiritualstrengthshealing.com where you can take the SSHP online.

In addition to showing you your six premier spiritual strengths, the power in you, the SSHP also identifies one shadow and one compulsion for each of your six spiritual strengths. Both shadows and compulsions are human vulnerabilities that can pull you away from your spiritual center—creating something of an imbalance in you. You will learn a wealth of information about yourself in the 20-page profile that accompanies the SSHP—the backbone of the *Spiritual Strengths Healing Plan*. You will not want to be without the insight it provides.

When you're armed with the personal wisdom detailed in your SSHP results, you can then begin to open yourself more fully to the special caregiver grace that I believe is available to you. Your spiritual strengths illuminate your mind, strengthen your heart, bolster your resolve, and activate your decisions so you can enter onto a new plane of caregiving where you find: new peace of mind and heart, new hope to carry on fully, new vision to see all the good in your care receiver and yourself, new steadfastness to stay engaged, new empathy so you can understand your care receiver and yourself as you never have before, new power to make right choices, and a new commitment to carry on even in the face of fear and danger.

There is no substitute for a strong personality in your caregiving. Nothing is stronger than an illuminated mind and a resolute spirit that is anointed by the most potent power on earth or heaven— the grace of your spiritual strengths. Harness your strengths, capture your innate energy, and embrace what is your inheritance.

Everything that you believe, perceive, think, feel, decide, and act all originates, is processed by, and is accomplished through your personality. Your personality is your 24 X 7 sentinel, your incoming and outgoing traffic control command center, your computer central processing switching assembly, your data operating system, your think tank, feelings sensitivity receptor site, your decisions headquarters, and your actions accelerator. It's all this and more; without a personality you wouldn't function.

When you walk into a room you bring your beliefs, attitudes, and values along with you in your believing function of your personality. You peruse or scan the room with your perceiving function. You make evaluations and assessment about the room with your thinking function; you even have immediate emotional connections about the room in your feelings function. You make choices, see options, and make plans about the room with your deciding function, and you execute actions about the room with your acting function. You do all this hardly aware that all this is going on.

## Personality and Caregiving

Think of all the beliefs, perceptions, thoughts, feelings, decisions, and actions that go into your caregiving. Your personality does a lot of work, and the big question here is: who is in charge of your personality? It's easy to say that you are in charge of your own personality, but are you really? How aware are you that you can take firmer control of your personality? Your personality isn't supposed to "run" you; no, you are supposed to run your personality. Are you, or is your personality simply taking you for a ride?

*The more you can take control of your personality, the more successful you will be in all your caregiving and the more personally meaningful it will be for you.*

So how do you gain a better control of and therefore more effective use of your personality? The answer comes from the deepest part of you—your spiritual center...your soul. Your soul is the touch-point between here and eternity, between you and God. Your soul is the gateway through which all grace (God's power and might) flows into you. Open your soul's gateway and the power of God's grace is yours.

Your personality has already been gifted with God's grace. You have received a special facet of the infinite diamond of God's grace in each of the six functions of your personality. This grace, which we call your spiritual strengths, provides the power to "run" your personality. Most people don't realize that they have this power, and that they can intentionally harness this power in their everyday lives.

Once you come to realize that your primary caregiving goal is to learn how to love better, and you take the SSHP, then you will arrive at a much clearer understanding of how to put into practice the remaining nine caregiving principles described in this book. Here is your overall caregiving vision—to better learn your innate strengths, to become more your true self that God made you to be as a consequence of walking the *caregiving* path that you've been given.

Caregiving becomes your coat of many colors, your hero's journey, your personality animation, and your illumination mission that together bring you to an entirely new realization of the "authentic you." When seen through the eyes of your soul, you can easily recognize that caregiving brings you to new heights of self-awareness, and a dramatically new appreciation of the gift of life you've been given.

Without question, your personality, enriched by the spiritual strengths you've been given, is your most important and powerful caregiving tool. When you walk into the caregiving room with your spiritually-energized personality, whether it's a home setting, a care center, or a hospital room, you bring your beliefs, values, and attitudes of enlightenment. You bring new and holy vision. You bring a celestial understanding of what's really happening here. You bring sweet emotions of love. You bring sacred choices. You bring actions that reflect the divinity of your spiritual strengths. Together you bring an abundance of Spirit that makes you glow. Certainly this is the ideal; but you can't be so personality aware 24 X 7.

You are, after all, still quite human. You are broken (as we all are), and you can and do make mistakes. You do bring your personality shadows and compulsions with you, although, with a new-found understanding of your personality, your life is forever changed—ever more healthy, happy, and holy because you have found a way in your *caregiving* to express the "trueness" of you, your heart's desire, the power of the universe—you have been made brand new!

*Because I care, I remain faithful to my role and my experience.*

# Caregiving Principle Two

You Cannot Honor Your Care Receiver by
Dishonoring Yourself or Your Loved Ones

Illness of any sort, body, mind, or spirit, can be pernicious. It attacks the body and eats at the soul; it scavenges and destroys. Illness can be like a terrorist in the night, and it's horrendous in its effects. Even the treatments our modern medical community has devised, while stupendous, are also scary, time consuming, overwhelmingly expensive, bodily invasive, emotionally devastating, and soul wrenching. The very word "illness" evokes an immediate and noxious reaction in us that sucks our breath away and pulls us into a vortex of fear.

With this unfolding panorama as an emotional backdrop, caregivers can become caught up in the mammoth cause at hand, and react to the call with a zeal and passion motivated by a mixture of emotions heretofore unknown. Caregivers can throw themselves into the fray much like foot soldiers marching off to meet an invading enemy. Captured by a fervent furor in their attempts and commitment to help honor the afflicted one, they can, without the benefit of self-awareness, dishonor themselves and do the same to their loved ones. Eventually this process wears them down; it diminishes them and throws them into an unstable state much less than their resources and strengths would normally support. As wounded casualties, they are vulnerable to attack. They can even suffer a post-caregiving stress marked by an odd mixture of their shadows and compulsions that creates confusion and weakness. In short, they lose themselves and become—in ways both unique and common—ineffective. The battle fatigue can, in some cases, become so paralyzing that they have no other option but to take themselves offline.

## Honor and Caregiving

What does honor mean in the caregiving setting? Certainly it can't mean "obey." Your care receiver sometimes wishes for things that you cannot oblige them—you cannot obey all requests in a simplistic obedience. Honor does possess strong overtones of "respect." In the caregiving arena, respect means recognizing the uniqueness of your care receiver and acting in ways which fully honor that person as a unique individual who is made, quite purposefully by God, to be just who he or she is.

Respect is that human relationship condition created when each partner, caregiver and care receiver, clearly sees the uniqueness of the other. Respect means coming to genuinely know, appreciate, and even honor the specialness of your care receiver as a manifestation of God's love and care. Respect means that you suspend any judgment about what you may not like about your care receiver. Respect means that you accept the personal idiosyncrasies or quirks of your care receiver and try to give affirmation to her on a daily basis. Without respect, there is no honoring; and without respect, the relationship destroyer of resentment can find room to wiggle in.

If you are a spouse or family caregiver, then you have tons of emotional and historical background that accompanies you into caregiving. Some of this background may fit into a category commonly called "baggage." This could include: regrets, blame, guilt, disappointments, so-called "unfinished business," anger, resentments, and the like that provide a messy yet unspoken undercurrent to the *caregiving* relationship. Yet, spouses and family members also offer brighter and personality-bolstering characteristics such as: humble appreciation, deep love, tender thoughtfulness, and wondrous gratitude. Such sentiment seasons the illness care relationship with poignant ingredients that grandly facilitates care and makes it dramatically meaningful.

If your care receiver is a stranger to you, you still, by a process known in psychology as *transference*, associate a mountain of connections, associations, assumptions, and conceptions that emerge from your believing function of your personality, and which you project onto your illness care receiver. You also mix in your beliefs about caregiving into the "batter" of your foundational understanding of your role *vis a vis* your care receiver. Some caregivers make the illogical jump that because they are performing tasks that seem fundamentally parental, that they should quite naturally assume a parent-child role with the caregiver as the parent and the care receiver as the child. This, as you might imagine, can be most damaging to the whole enterprise of caregiving to both parties.

### Caregiving Characterized by Honor Brings Unexpected Riches

A fundamental principle of this book is that caregiving brings unexpected riches. The gifts and benefits that you accrue from successfully honoring your care receiver may not be as tangible as monetary riches, but they are true sources of all wealth nonetheless. Riches such as patience, perseverance, stamina, hope, mercy, and charity all flow into caregivers who find ways to honor their care receivers more and more deeply. On the other hand, dishonor doesn't bring physical death but an inner death to parts of ourselves; we experience loss of honor, self-respect, and peace of mind. Dishonor brings death to our relationships— making them lifeless and shallow. Consequently, we miss out on a fundamental form of spiritual and psychological nourishment that gives life. The degree to which we dishonor, we deal "death messages" to our own sense of self.

What does make sense as a guidepost for honoring our care receiver, without dishonoring ourselves, is the notion of "do not abandon." *Abandon* may seem a strong word, and yet I find it accurate for many caregiving situations. We may not abandon our care receiver physically, but we can abandon them in other ways. Abandonment means to withdraw protection, support, or help, or to exercise complete disinterest in the fate of the one cared for. Abandonment is clearly an extreme form of dishonoring. But like all violations of God's laws, abandonment also dishonors those who do the abandoning.

Abandonment is a rather imprecise word. What would be considered abandonment by one caregiver would be quite natural for another. Each caregiving situation needs to be appraised individually to determine if any abandonment exists. In any event, abandonment can be expressed on many levels such as—

- Physical abandonment: neglect of physical needs.
- Financial abandonment: failure to fund basic needs.
- Emotional abandonment: very little, if any, close contact.
- Psychological abandonment: verbal abuse or neglect.
- Familial abandonment: cut off from family involvement.
- Spiritual abandonment: making no reference to God or the hereafter.

You show honor to your care receiver by your willingness to share your gifts and talents (your spiritual strengths) with her. These gifts are not simply the physical tasks that you perform but equally important they include your respect, your esteem, and even a reverence.

However, you are never called to abandon yourself in the caregiving honoring process. Some caregivers become worn down to their very last ounce of energy, and instead of heeding the cue that they now need to care for themselves; they go ahead and give that last ounce away. They are left with nothing; they are emotionally spent; their energies are all but exclusively devoted to their care receiver. This may be necessary in extreme times of need, but such a situation cannot persist over the long haul. Some caregivers can abandon themselves in much the same way that care receivers can be abandoned:

- Physical abandonment: neglect of one's own physical needs.

- Financial abandonment: failure to fund one's basic needs.

- Emotional abandonment: very little, if any, contact with friends.

- Psychological abandonment: constant negative self-talk or neglect toward oneself.

- Familial abandonment: cut off from own family involvement.

- Spiritual abandonment: forfeiture of one's faith and prayer.

When honoring is not a plank in the platform of your caregiving efforts, dishonor always fills the void. Dishonor in any forms causes an erosion of your very life energy. You lose the potency of your spiritual strengths leaving you bereft of self-honor, self-respect, and peace of mind. Dishonor leaves you lifeless and shallow. You lose that essential psychological and spiritual nourishment that gives you life...you cut yourself off from the power of God's grace. When you dishonor, usually without consciously knowing it, you move out of your personality spiritual strengths and into your shadows and/or compulsions.

## A Scale of Caregiving

The following scale helps you gauge the degree of honor (or dishonor) that may be present in your caregiving work.

### 1. Violence or Active Abuse

Inflicting some form of violence upon your care receiver in the form of physical, mental, or verbal abuse.

### 2. Abandonment or Neglect

Withholding protection or support from your care receiver, allowing life-threatening situations to persist.

### 3. Indifference or Disengagement

Displaying poorly-concealed indifference or deep irritation toward your care receiver...maintaining an air of detachment, disengagement, or aloofness toward your care receiver...regarding care you give as only troublesome obligation.

### 4. General Support

Freely giving support to your care receiver, even though this care may be given with a somewhat guarded degree of warmth and respect; you do show concern for your care receiver's emotional, physical, and spiritual well-being.

### 5. Expressed Empathy and a Quality Relationship

Striving to create a healthy relationship between you and your care receiver, where thoughts and feelings can be freely expressed and received with nonjudgmental and mutual positive regard.  Demonstrating the relationship quality of "being with" your care receiver on an emotional level.

### 6. Sympathy

Feeling sorry for your care receiver; deeply regretting that he is suffering the losses that illness brings.

### 7. Occasional Over-Involvement

Periodic attempts to "do for" rather than to "be with" your care receiver.

### 8. Consistent Over-Involvement

Thinking and worrying about your care receiver all the time...being compulsively driven to do more and more for your care receiver...an inability to stop.

### 9. Heroic Over-Involvement

Caregiving that is characterized by frantic and desperate attempts to provide for your care receiver's every possible need and want—leaving you, the caregiver equally frantic and desperate.

Where are you on this scale of *caregiving*?

- Items 1, 2, and 3 describe various degrees of dishonoring one's care receiver.

- Items 4, 5, and 6 describe degrees of caregiving balance.

- Items 7, 8, and 9 describe varying degrees of dishonoring yourself as the caregiver.

The ideal caregiving "posture" is one that emphasizes items 4, 5, and 6. When you strive to center yourself in your spiritual strengths, you are automatically moving yourself toward a healthy point of balance, a "place" where your caregiving expresses your best, and equally important, a "place where you are not over-taxing yourself" either. Staying in your spiritual strengths gives you a marvelous internal balance where you can function optimally both for your care receiver and for yourself.

*Because I care, I try to remain "light and bright" with my care receiver.*

# Caregiving Principle Three

## Distinguish between Your Care Receiver's Actual Care Requirements and Her/his Personal Desires

Your care receiver's care requirements can loom like an advancing storm, a wall of dark clouds that threaten to simply overrun your caregiving capacities. At times you may run out of time or energy, or both, and find yourself overtaken in the unending torrent of caregiving needs: personal needs, medical needs, financial needs, relationship needs...need upon need threaten to sweep you up into the rising flood. Certainly all these needs seem to be requirements...but are they? Might some not be obligatory demands? Might some of your care receiver's "needs" only masquerade as requirements when actually they are but "wants"—simple desires that have little or no real necessity attached to them at all?

As I observe caregivers operating in a host of caregiving settings—home care, residential care, skilled care, and even hospital care—one disturbing dynamic of care that appears to be endemic is caregiver burnout. Of all the many factors that contribute to this burnout, perhaps the most confounding one is how caregivers confuse "wants" and "needs."

Caregivers seem naturally dedicated to detecting and dealing with needs as they arise in their care receivers. Their selfless service is exemplary and even inspirational at times. However, there is no compelling motivation to be equally diligent in addressing requests of care receivers that fall into the category of "wants." As they experience successive losses, some care receivers can become emotionally very needy. While some of this neediness is genuine; whole other parts are subconscious attempts to keep their caregivers close at hand as a means of increasing emotional security. The care receivers begin to increase their care requests, and can even transform these "wants" into demands.

The response you, as the caregiver, make to these sometimes flattering and other times strident requests can make all the difference as to whether these "want" requests continue or erode away. Caregivers need to discern between requests that are needs and those that are only wants. The degree to which this caregiving task is not accomplished is the same degree to which caregivers can find themselves adrift on a sea of uncertainty, and risk being pulled under in an ever stronger whirlpool of requests that have no basis in actual need.

You must remain mindful of the difference between need and want by asking yourself such questions as: "What will happen if this request is not granted?" or "How will my care receiver's life change for the better if I satisfy this request?" And perhaps the most important question of all, "Will I further infantilize my care receiver if I meet this request?" Infantilization means "becoming like a child." You can unwittingly take your care receiver's integrity away if you consistently regard their every request as your command for perfection. In addition, such behavior is your surest route to burnout.

### *Try to Stay Out of the Middle*

Caregivers frequently find themselves in the middle of their care receiver and—

- The medical community and attendant to insurance paperwork.
- Siblings who mean well but who can be cumbersome and tedious at times.
- Community agencies that offer services.
- Legal professionals and personnel.
- Utility companies.
- Retail establishments.
- Friends and neighbors.
- Church and religious personnel.

Being in the middle creates its own frustration. Trying to arrange, manage, and otherwise balance all the "business" of your care receiver, as well as all their needs and wants, can gradually pile up layers of stress that can eventually overwhelm even the most diligent and organized caregiver. This in-the-middle position doesn't happen overnight; rather it builds up gradually and unintentionally, until the caregiver is shocked into an awakening of the new reality. It's at this point that remedial help is needed.

Naturally the much more preferable "fix" is to prevent the in-the-middle position from emerging in the first place. To accomplish this, the caregiver needs to survey all six of their life arenas and be mindful of retaining their overall life structure as best as they can. Keeping your life structure as balanced as possible is vital for personal stability. Try to arrange help when and where you can so you can remain connected in what's been life giving for you. The six life arenas are—

- <u>Work or Life Cause</u>. While it's easy to say that you need to continue investing in your career and/or avocation even during your caregiving time, the reality of how to do this is confounding. If you're still in the paid-work world, maintain your position if at all possible. It provides an outlet and a grounding that remains an important part of your life. The same remains true if you're involved in volunteer work, or an avocation.

- <u>Family</u>. Keep your presence in and focus on your family. While your care receiver may be a family member, try to ensure constant contact with your own family. Nothing replaces family for continuity of support and generative understanding. Sometimes family relationships can become conflicted or lead to misunderstanding, but it's important to keep the lines of communication open and operative.

- <u>Friends</u>. Friends give stability and surety, support and understanding during this perilous time. Accept their help; call them even if you have nothing to say...they will help you.

- <u>Self</u>. Maintaining a healthy relationship with your self is paramount for optimal caregiving success. What are your internal messages to yourself? What are you telling yourself about you and your performance as a caregiver? Try to separate fact from fiction, and reality from fantasy. So often we find that caregivers are their own worst enemies in that they subject themselves to a constant internal barrage of illusionary negativism, almost insisting that they are doing an inadequate job. Personality awareness (chapter one) is a constant requirement. The other side of the "Self" life arena is care of your body. If you don't exercise regularly...it's time to start! Nothing replaces a good diet, adequate sleep, stress reduction, moderate alcohol use, and exercise for keeping strong and vigorous.

- <u>Leisure</u>. Don't neglect your leisure. Whatever your leisure interests were before your new caregiving career—whether through active involvement in exercise or sports, social interaction, intellectual stimulation, spectator appreciation, or just "hanging out" —it's mandatory that you keep up these activities as much as you can.

- <u>Faith</u>. Strengthen your faith life. Your faith is to your ongoing development what sails are to a ship...not a burden but a means of power. One of the themes of this book is that caregiving is yet another chapter in the full unfolding of the true you; caregiving is a curriculum of personal and spiritual development. Remain open to its instruction, inspiration, mystery, and delight...caregiving has it all. It's a coat of many colors that brings with it the abundance that we've been promised. It's poignant and painful, touching and tedious, profound and pitiful, and it's energizing and exasperating. The one constant through it all is God.

## Acknowledge the Losses, but Don't Get Caught up in "Feeling Sorry"

A common mistake made by novice caregivers is to be in a constant state of "feeling sorry." While illness is so often wrapped in difficulty, pain, and even tragedy, it's decidedly unhelpful for you to lapse into a "feeling sorry" reaction toward your care receiver. You will eventually buckle under the emotional pressure of helplessness if you can't shake off "feeing sorry."

I know that some days seem like a cascade of losses that can never be "righted." The losses seem so pervasive and deep that there seems no recovery. Caregiving calls you to confront the losses, look them straight in the face, stand toe-to-toe with them...and remember that loss is the driving force of all human growth. Without loss, you wouldn't grow at all. Caregiving forces hard lessons of loss, and consequently a very hard growth. Yet, if you avoid the loss, or catastrophize the loss, making it the central focus of your caregiving, you lose your perspective of integrity and forfeit your connection to God. Sometimes there simply is no other place to go but on your knees.

Feeling sorry is a sympathetic reaction. Sympathy is most appropriate in wakes and funerals, but not in the healthy caregiving relationship. Sympathy is reacting to another's distress with your own feelings and your own emotions. Sympathy focuses on you and not on your care receiver (where your emotions belong).

Empathy is far preferable to sympathy. Enlightened caregivers use empathy—which involves reflecting back to your care receiver the emotions they just displayed. Empathy places the focus of the interchange where it needs to be...on your care receiver. Sympathy says, in effect, *"I'm stuck in my own emotions of sorrow,"* while empathy says, *"I'm fully with you and your emotions."* Sympathy has the unwanted effect of diminishing your care receiver, while empathy builds her up.

## Be Cautious of Creating Over-Dependence

Disease itself, and especially the treatment of disease, can bring about radical changes in how your care receiver sees himself. It's very easy to lose a former sense of being capable and self-reliant in the face of illness. Depression is a common attendant feeling as confidence in oneself fades. Sometimes your care receiver feels so diminished that she appears incapable of making even the smallest decision. In situations where your care receiver succumbs to the gradual diminishing of self, it's common that you might step up your care to compensate. It's altogether common to over-step the line from giving increased care to over-giving and creating what mental health practitioners would call "infantilization." Infantilization is a condition where your care receiver becomes psychologically unable of doing almost anything for himself—even when the capacity to perform such tasks on his own remains intact. Continue to let your care receiver do as much as she can for herself—even when it might be somewhat hard to do so.

## Try to Keep the Relationship as Balanced as Possible

Because of the debility of most care receivers, we sometimes see an emotionally lopsided relationship emerge between the caregiver and the care receiver. A lopsided relationship is one where all the emotional work of the relationship is accomplished by the caregiver, with little or no input or emotional energy coming from the care receiver. Such lopsided relationships breed either guilt and depression, on the one hand, or anger and emotional distance on the other. Try to allow your care receiver to offer input and emotional energy into the relationship. Try to encourage care receivers to talk, to self-disclose, to be themselves even in the smallest ways; try to let them keep their own individual personality intact as much as you can.

## Educate Yourself

Persons with illness have ongoing needs that fall into three categories:

- Physical or materials needs.
- Emotional, psychosocial, or psychological needs.
- Spiritual needs.

No individual caregiver can possibly attend to all these needs. Caregivers need to be care managers as much as they need to offer direct care. Caregivers need to educate themselves about available resources and make intentional efforts to bring these services to the care receiver. There exists an ever-widening network of care and care support services specially organized to meet the needs of persons with illness and their caregivers. Such programs are organized on several levels: town, city, county, state and federal in the public sector, and associations, institutes, and faith-based organizations in the private sector.

One of the best sources of information is your public library. A good reference librarian can be an invaluable resource. Beyond the library, get online. Your first stop is the American Cancer Society or ACS, and many other disease specific organizations. Most of these organizations not only offer services directly, they also serve as a clearinghouse for services that can be found in the surrounding community. A call to them for an informational appointment is a "must" for any caregiver. Your local hospitals are also excellent sources of information and services, as are faith- based organizations such as Catholic Charities, Lutheran Family and Children Services, and many others religious denominations that offer similar services of varying degrees.

### *Emotional Needs*

Caregiving can sometimes focus so much on the physical sickness and the treatment through the medical community that we forget the equally important aspects of our emotions. Here are some standard emotional needs of all persons. As you read through these, try to relate them to both your care receiver AND yourself.

- <u>Have a sense of self-worth</u>. I am a person of dignity and I deserve respect.

- <u>Possess at least one close friend</u>. Having a confidant enhances happiness.

- <u>Feel productive</u>. I still have the capacity to "do" something.

- <u>Feel useful</u>. There are people 'out there' who believe that I am productive and a useful member of society.

- Feel treated as a unique individual. I refuse to become a 'patient' in the sense that it's my new identity. I am always something more than a patient…something more than a caregiver.

- Possess a meaningful sense of belonging. I belong to a group that loves me…a family…a church community…and more.

- Have control of decision-making. There are still some things that I can decide; I am not totally dependent on others to meet all my needs right now.

- Overcome loneliness. Being lonely is devastating…it robs one of a sense of being, it sets one adrift in a confusing and unknown sea, it's disorienting and destabilizing.

## Dealing with Loss

Loss is ubiquitous when we operate in the illness arena. In one sense, illness and caregiving is about how one handles loss. The very first way of successfully handling loss is changing your attitude about it. Most of our beliefs about loss revolve around negativism. We see loss as "bad," as something to be avoided or triumphed over, protected from, ensured against, or simply ignored. This is unfortunate because notions like these only bring frustration, regret, resentment, and depression into the caregiving walk for both the care receiver and the caregiver.

Our shortsighted view of loss prevents us from understanding the essential truth about loss: loss is the driving force of all human growth. In fact, we only grow when we lose! Examples of this paradox are everywhere in our lives. We had to give up, or lose, our toddlerhood before we could enter into the stage of early childhood; we had to lose adolescence in order to move on to early adulthood; we had to lose our forties to dive into our fifties. So goes the developmental imperative of the human condition.

How many times have you looked back on an event that you at first thought to be horrendous, only to later completely reverse your perspective when you realized that this initially-lamentable event actually brought a cornucopia of good things to your life? Loss, while noxious at first, is the mechanism we humans use to move on in life, to grow, to become better. It's hard to think of the ponderous and excruciating losses that illness can bring as anything that could possibly advance our growth, yet such a notion deserves attention.

When it's just about impossible to see any good coming from the loss, it's ever more important to hold on to the realization of what you can and can't do. It's impossible for you to prevent the loss, circumvent the loss, "fix" the loss, or otherwise erase the loss from the palate of your, or your care receiver's life. What you can do is recognize that although you can't change the circumstances surrounding the loss, nor the loss itself, you do have almost absolute power over how you interpret this "loss event" and how you can draw energy from it rather than letting it drain you.

Adapting to and coping with the multiple losses of illness are the primary developmental tasks that persons with illness and their caregivers must face.

How do you, as a concerned and loving illness caregiver, keep your own composure and not be overcome with false guilt that you feel that your own life is being controlled by caregiving? You cannot deal with the losses themselves, but only with the emotional reactions to these losses.

Some of the most common emotional reactions to loss include: anxiety, fear, fright, anger, resentment, and even contempt. These are very common reactions experienced by many illness caregivers (as well as persons with illness). Have you ever felt confused, disoriented, or guilty? Have you ever withdrawn into yourself, gotten depressed, or even become slightly paranoid?

You are not alone. These are common emotional reactions to loss among caregivers.

So you have two big tasks to accomplish when illness begins to usher in a host of losses. The first is to realize that you cannot "right" the "wrong" of illness for your care receiver. The only thing you can do is to recognize the intense feelings your care receiver is experiencing as their reaction to the losses and focus on these feelings. The second is to realize that you too are experiencing feelings of varying intensity as a consequence to the losses you are witnessing. You too are called to see these feelings as common, and not as some indication that you are somehow doing a sub-standard job at caregiving.

## Always Operate From Your Spiritual Strengths

Again, your job constantly requires you to deal with your own thoughts and feelings by tracing them back to your shadows or compulsions (where they originated), and shift these thoughts back to your spiritual strengths. Your spiritual strengths provide you with all the power and might, perseverance, and stamina to continue—even in the face of fear, doubt, uncertainty, loss, disillusionment, and all the other emotions and forces that can work against you. Your spiritual strengths are your connection to the great I AM.

*Because I care, I honor my care receiver as a unique rendition of the Spirit's grace.*

# Caregiving Principle Four

## Construct a Quality Relationship with Your Care Receiver

What is at the core of caregiving? Is caregiving primarily performing tasks, completing chores, and ticking off items on a to-do list? Or, is caregiving essentially an unfolding process of building relationship? This question is the fulcrum between care that is merely functional, and care that is relational and healing.

Is your primary focus on what needs to be done for your care receiver, or is the person of your care receiver your primary focus? The difference between these two approaches to caregiving has direct impact on you. One approach will ultimately make you into a caregiving automaton; the other will bring you into the grand drama of the profound transition that expresses ever-new colors as it unfurls its beauty and its beastliness— sometimes at the same time. Relationship not only moves the drama of life, it also enriches, enhances, enables, and envelops you. In the end, what you gather up and keep in your heart and soul are not all the completed tasks, but the fuller measure of the relationship that comes alive in the process of completing the tasks of care.

### Six Relationship Essentials

A quality caregiving relationship is characterized by the following six essentials:

- <u>Togetherness</u>. Each person shares a genuine sense of unity or connection.
- <u>Respect</u>. Each person's "personhood" is given freedom of expression.
- <u>Communication</u>. Each person listens, listens, listens, and listens some more.
- <u>Intimacy</u>. Each person exhibits warmth and devotion toward the other.
- <u>Trust</u>. Each person exhibits personal reliability toward the other.
- <u>Commitment</u>. Each person practices wanting to be <u>at</u> and <u>on</u> each other's side.

When these six are brought to their highest, most spiritual level, they transform into something quite unexpected. These six conditions (described below) form the sacred goals for the quality caregiving relationship. Remember, these six are *ideals*, which means that they can never be fully achieved. Please don't lament that these conditions are not fully present in your *caregiving*. Growing toward these ideals is an ongoing process that never really ends, but is well worth the struggle. The key to becoming whole is not necessarily to achieve wholeness, but to develop the willingness to be whole each and every day of your life.

### Togetherness Becomes Sacred Unity

Sacred Unity is a spiritual relationship condition created when each partner—caregiver and care receiver—knows without question that the relationship is an emerging diamond of wholeness attempting to reflect the light of God.

### Respect Becomes Blessed Uniqueness

Blessed Uniqueness is the spiritual relationship condition created when each partner—caregiver and care receiver—sees and recognizes her own spiritual strengths in all six functions of her personality, which allows for a fuller flowering of spiritual distinctiveness and wholeness in the union.

### Communication Becomes Transcendent Prayerfulness

Transcendent Prayerfulness is the spiritual relationship condition created when each partner—caregiver and care receiver—thinks of the relationship as an ongoing communication with God and therefore becomes for both a journey of faith with God.

### Intimacy Becomes Holy Groundedness

Holy Groundedness is the spiritual relationship condition created when each partner—caregiver and care receiver—feels a sense of stability coming from a deeply-seated sharing between the two and God (i.e., they feel their relationship is holy ground).

### Trust Becomes Redeeming Forgiveness

Redeeming Forgiveness is the spiritual relationship condition created when each partner—caregiver and care receiver—chooses to let God's healing absolution permeate them to the center.

### Commitment Becomes Sacred Faithfulness

Sacred Faithfulness is the spiritual relationship condition created when each partner—caregiver and care receiver—acts with certainty that God is the center of the relationship, making it a holy bond.

## Beware of Over-Commitment

Having just enumerated the ideals of a fully- functioning *caregiving* relationship, and identifying one of the ideals as commitment, I now give you a caution to be wary of over-commitment. Over-commitment is perhaps the most common failing of caregivers...some caregivers think they can, and should, do anything and everything. Such over-commitment erodes the fullness of the unfolding relationship because it stifles the effectiveness and undermines the efficiency of the relationship's development. Perhaps the best way for you to avoid over-commitment is to embrace the ten fundamentals for an effective caregiving relationship described in this book.

## Develop a Quality Relationship

What is a quality relationship? First we need to see what a quality relationship is not, and build from there. There are three relationships that unenlightened caregivers may lapse into when they lack the skills and understanding they require. These three relationships are almost universal in our culture and, because they are internalized so deeply in each of us, we can withdraw into them when we are stymied or reach an impasse in our caregiving attempts. These three are—

- The supervisor—employee relationship.
- The teacher—student relationship.
- The parent—child relationship.

Each of these three differs in style, purpose, and goals from a quality caregiving relationship, and yet because we know them so well we are at risk of taking one or the other as our model for caregiving. In doing so, we undermine the effectiveness of illness care.

## Quality vs. Quantity Caregiving Relationship

We are tempted to see relationship as a means of getting the most done in the shortest time. This is a common caregiving mistake and often kills the possibility of creating a truly facilitative relationship because it all but nullifies the emotional bond so necessary for true relationship to emerge. The following table describes some differences between a quality relationship and a quantity relationship. Try to identify which kind of relationship you are constructing with your care receiver.

| Quality Relationship | Quantity Relationship |
| --- | --- |
| Being with | Doing for |
| Emotional closeness | Emotional distance |
| Warmth | Being aloof |
| Fostering independence | Fostering dependence |
| A person-focused perspective | Problem-focused perspective |
| A feelings-oriented atmosphere | Thing-oriented atmosphere |
| Mutual equality | Dominance and submission |

## Goals of a Facilitative Caregiving Relationship

Obviously the goal is to move as close to the quality *caregiving* relationship end of the spectrum as possible. Having such a relationship—

- Fosters positive mental health. Emotional adjustment, ability to make and keep friends, ability to accept responsibility, ability to maintain personal independence, and calmness of action.

- <u>Promotes personal effectiveness</u>. The caregiver helps the care receiver not just survive but thrive. The caregiver encourages, affirms, and supports.

- <u>Encourages decision-making</u>. Help care receivers identify and make decisions according to their ability.

- <u>Expands knowledge of health and wellness</u>. The caregiver provides basic knowledge about the physical, emotional, psychological, and spiritual changes going on.

- <u>Assists in problem resolution</u>. The caregiver facilitates in making sound decisions.

- <u>Enhances behavior changes</u>. The illness journey is about change and growth. The caregiver frames all change as growth in some way.

- <u>Promotes self-advocacy</u>. The caregiver allows the care receiver to speak for herself whenever possible.

---

*Become increasing aware of the language you use both with your care receiver and with yourself.*
*The Three General Characteristics of a Quality Relationship*

---

### Be Genuine

Genuineness is your ability to share yourself in a manner that is open, natural, sincere, and nondirective. Authenticity, being who you truly are, is central to genuineness. Genuineness means being open and honest about your own needs, and not to forget them among the many caregiving challenges that swirl around you. Certainly you want to be attentive to your care receiver's needs, but you must remember your own as well.

The goal of genuineness is mutual trust—working hard to drop pretense and defense. When you can do this, your care receiver becomes more likely to follow along with you. Don't give internal excuses about your care receiver by saying to yourself things like: *"Oh, he's never expressed his feeling before; he's not going to start now."* Or, *"I can't be honest with her, she's too sick to understand."* Such illusionary statements block the condition of genuineness from entering into the relationship; they smother the opportunity for going emotionally deeper than your care receiver needs to in this hour of need.

### Be Compassionate

Compassionate caregiving is empathic: it zeroes in on the care receiver as the singular focus of the relationship. Compassion is the second trait of a quality caregiving relationship. Compassion includes your ability to recognize fully what your care receiver is trying to communicate—to understand "where your care receiver is" emotionally—and to see the world as they do. This isn't at all easy. To be compassionate is not being sympathetic. Sympathy means that you express your own emotions about the unfortunate circumstances your care receiver is dealing with. Sympathy can actually be damaging in that you are communicating an, "I'm sorry for your loss" attitude that ultimately inhibits healthy, quality caregiving.

When you are compassionate, you are not trying to solve or "fix" anything; you are not trying to come to any kind of decisions. You are simply saying that you understand your care receiver's feelings, you comprehend what they are saying in the fullness of their communications...you are empathetic not sympathetic.

### Be Care-ful...Be Respectful

Let your care receiver be the person whom she is. Honor even those things you might not like about your care receiver. Being care-ful, respectful, and maintaining unconditional positive regard toward your care receiver is the attitude that accepts the right of your care receiver to think and to feel the way she wishes. Your respect says, *"It's OK, I understand you. I'm not going to impose any of my standards upon you. You can do and think and feel and choose what you think is right and not have to concern yourself with what I may think is right."* Care-fullness has no hint of judgment, criticism, or disapproval; there is no arguing, threatening, ridiculing, rejecting, or belittling—you only give affirmation and acceptance.

A quality caregiving relationship is not cheap or quick. It is not shallow, nor is it easy...it takes enormous work and patience. This fourth principle provides a path you can walk with your care receiver. The path is sometimes rocky and hilly, but it leads to a land of honor, a land where peace and harmony prevail in an atmosphere made confident and bright by the light of the Spirit.

*Because I care, I look for ways of being fully present to my care receiver.*

# Caregiving Principle Five

## Caregiving is Essentially a Process of Enacting Well-Considered Choices

Good caregiving is mostly a matter of informed decision-making based on the best information available to you. Naturally, every care receiver is different in so very many ways, as is every caregiving setting. Yet, one theme that runs through every person and every setting is the requirement to make choices. Caregiving would be ever so much easier if there were an agreed upon formula, a set of established procedures, universal time tables, and unwavering (and simple) techniques that could be applied in all situations. Unfortunately this isn't the case. Caregiving involves a continuous conveyor belt, an almost endless flood of choices, choices, and more choices. Your decisions on a minute-by-minute, hour-by-hour, and day-by-day basis are fundamental requirements of caregiving.

Without a doubt, you attitude (personality function number one) about illness in general, and also about caregiving as a human role, play heavily into the way you go about your caregiving day. Perhaps you'd like to take this little quiz as a sort of primer for this chapter. The following questions are answered by a simple "yes" or "no." Try to answer them with all illness patients in mind and not just your own care receiver.

## Characteristics of Persons with Illness

| Y/N | Persons with illness— |
|-----|------------------------|
|  | Are on a downward slope. |
|  | Worry about everything they shouldn't. |
|  | Feel sorry for themselves. |
|  | Eventually become selfish. |
|  | Are dependent. |
|  | Are irritable and cranky. |
|  | Like to be waited on. |
|  | Are depressed most of the time. |
|  | Generally bad patients. |
|  | Have lost their "spark." |
|  | Tend to mask their feelings. |
|  | Take everything for granted. |
|  | Make things so complex. |
|  | Are arrogant. |
|  | Are helpless. |

How did you do?  While each of these 15 descriptors could apply to some persons with illness, certainly not all persons with illness would conform to all of these negative statements. The point of the simple little "quiz" is only to stimulate your thinking about attitudes, because your attitudes as a caregiver are the "mother" of your actions.

## Two Types of Choices

As a caregiver, you make two kinds of choices: external and internal. **External choices** are primarily decisions about caregiving tasks. What needs to be done now? What is the best way to accomplish this task? Do I need help in performing this task? Should I do this now or later? Does this really need to be done today, or can it wait until tomorrow? Questions like these, and so many others, permeate the caregiving setting; they swirl around your head and require that you develop and engage effective executive skills to ensure all caregiving tasks are accomplished in a timely and efficient manner. External choices are a big part of the *caregiving* "territory."

**Internal choices** can be a bit more challenging because they speak not to "what" needs to be done (the task), but rather to the manner in which you will perform it. Internal choices require that you engage your primary caregiving tool—your spiritual personality. As the first *caregiving* principle clearly states: your spiritual personality, animated by your unique spiritual strengths, represent your most powerful caregiving tool. Your most import choice, then, is becoming increasingly aware of your spiritual personality, and then choosing to illuminate your caregiving by engaging your six unique spiritual strengths with intention.

The fundamental question here is, *"Am I operating out of my spiritual strengths, or out of my shadows and/or compulsions?"* While this question is never an easy one, your day-to-day and hour-to-hour answer to it not only guides your *caregiving*, but also determines what the entire endeavor of caregiving means for you—an experience of oppressive drudgery or one of soul inspiration! This choice is always yours to make. Your internal choices determine your psychological and emotional environment—an environment you carry inside your mind and heart as you go about your external environment making and executing all your caregiving tasks.

Decisions are required to bring about change. Healthy change requires strength, and strength is derived from your own sense of what's called personal power. Caregivers are called upon to address change on a daily basis. All change, especially change required for healing, requires an attitude of self-empowerment and self-agency...the ability to influence events as well as the capacity to be both resourceful and creative. Change also demands self-discipline and self-control—all ingredients of the deciding function of your personality. Decisions ensure that positive change actually becomes a working reality in your life.

Poor decisions originate in "poor" or illogical thinking. Your thoughts rocket through your entire nervous system; they determine how you mentally and emotionally process your caregiving endeavors. Your thinking is the fountain from which flow your feelings, decisions, and finally your actions. The better you can analyze your thoughts, the more you become aware whether they originate in your spiritual strengths, your shadows, or your compulsions. When your thoughts move toward your personal center, they speak from your most powerful, resourceful, and creative voice.

This little exercise may help you with this ongoing task. Look at each statement on the following page and try to determine to what extent it may be "at work" with you in your *caregiving*. You might want to actually rate each item on a scale of 1 to 10 (1 indicating that this statement is absolutely false for you, and 10 being that it is absolutely true for you, with numbers in between 1 and 10 indicating a relative placement of your true feelings about the statement) to get a clearer picture of how illogical thinking might be derailing your caregiving.

## Illness Care Statements

| | |
|---|---|
| | I cannot tolerate change in my care receiver. |
| | My care receiver doesn't do enough to help himself. |
| | My care receiver should be more kind and understanding of me. |
| | I should feel more positively toward my care receiver. |
| | I must obey my care receiver. |
| | I must find solutions for all situations that arise involving my care receiver. |
| | I'm ultimately "at fault" if anything goes wrong on my caregiving "watch." |
| | I'm simply not doing the caregiving job that I should be doing. |
| | I'm the one, perhaps the only one, who really knows what's best for my care receiver. |
| | I can never do enough for my care receiver. |

These 10 statements are attitudes...specifically, they are negative and paralyzing attitudes that will eventually distort your caregiving and contort your perceptions, thinking, and feelings about your role. The higher your scores, the more vulnerable you are to the noxious effects of these paralyzing attitudes. How did you do on this exercise? Did you develop any new insights about how you may be subconsciously thinking negatively toward your *caregiving* role?

### Choices about which You are Unaware

Actually you have many choices that you make on a minute-to-minute basis for which you may or may not be aware. These are internal decisions that determine more than any other decisions how you feel as you move through your caregiving day. As you read through the following decisions, ponder how you are currently resolving each one in your caregiving life. I pose these decisions as dialectics, as something vs. something else—because both sides of the dialectics are "working" on you. The question is which side will be stronger...which side will you "side" with as you go about your day? The choice is yours. Your spiritual strengths will always move you to the left side of the following inner-life decisions; your shadows and compulsions will move you over to the right side. We're hardly aware of the choices we have before us constantly, yet they become obvious when they're brought to light.

Each and every day, and each and every moment of your caregiving day, you have the power, indeed, the mandate, to choose between—

- The Holy Spirit vs. the World. The Holy Spirit, God's power moving within the world, is constantly nudging you to perceive God's love in the form of truth, beauty, and goodness as they find demonstration and fulfillment in your life. The world instructs the opposite: it "preaches" fear. For caregivers, this fear is manifested in many, many ways but commonly is displayed as insecurity, guilt, distress, sadness, anger, contention, discouragement, perfectionism, timidity, and the like. Eventually the pressure of all this is converted into the syndrome we call "burn-out."

- Wakefulness vs. Sleep. You are asleep to the degree that you don't awaken to the reality of your call. Part of your call today is being a caregiver. Fully awakening to this reality, as a call to love and ultimately to peace and self-fulfillment, is part of the choice you make every hour of your caregiving day.

- Forgiveness vs. Condemnation. When you forgive, you set yourself free; when you condemn, you confine yourself to an internal prison of self-degradation. No caregiver is perfect, none makes all the right decisions, none performs without flaw, or mistake, or accident, or misstep. Forgiveness, then, is a necessary part of any caregiving setting. Because shadows and compulsions "operate" within you, you are always called to forgive. You forgive yourself for all your commissions or omissions. Likewise, you forgive your care receiver for all of his "faults..." all that you condemn about him, all that he lacks, imposes, upsets, controls, manipulates, and the like.

- Love-finding vs. Fault-finding. You can choose to scan your caregiving horizon in search of faults to correct, or you can search for good things to celebrate. What you seek, you will find, because you will perceive what you believe is there. You will always find what you are looking for as long as your heart believes it is there.

- Peace vs. Turmoil. Perfect peace is, of course, not of this world, but you can inch closer and closer to peace as you find your center point in your spiritual strengths. Inner turmoil comes in many forms, but it all originates in your shadows and compulsions.

- <u>Freedom vs. Confinement</u>. The divine vision of this world offers freedom, while the world's view offers only bondage. Because you are first and foremost a child of God, you can be free from the fear and worry that the world offers. By seeing your brothers and sisters in the true light of the Spirit, you free yourself from the fear and guilt of condemnation. Judgment confines the soul, while love and peace offer freedom.

- <u>Joy and Well-Being vs. Fear</u>. Fear is usually your cry for help when you feel separated from yourself, from God. Joining the Divine through prayer, meditation, and right-mindedness is a way out of fear. You create your own fear when you choose to separate from your spiritual strengths. You cannot be "in love," in your spiritual strengths when your primary motivator is fear.

- <u>Meaning vs. Meaninglessness</u>. Without your spiritual strengths, you live in a meaningless world—a spinning carousel of nonsense. Without the meaning that God provides, you remain incomplete. In order to accept your purpose now, you cannot deny your spiritual strengths. You need to be fully awake to make the decision to accept your current purpose of caregiving. Accepting God's purpose brings joy to your heart and unity to your soul, as well as the holy recognition that you and your care receiver are truly one in spirit.

- <u>Truth vs. Error</u>. Truth gives life, indeed eternal life. When you choose truth, you drive out error. In order to comprehend truth, you must exercise faith. Choose truth and you will receive peace in your heart and progress in your mind. You will receive truth when you base your life on the highest forms of love—your spiritual strengths.

- Being Right vs. Being Happy. Being happy means choosing to let God share in your decisions. The world needs to be right, which is why it is characterized by criticism. Anger and condemnation are emotions that separate people, while forgiveness is the power for happiness.

- Being Forgiving vs. Being Unforgiving. Forgiveness is the bridge you walk across to happiness; without forgiveness you experience no happiness. The human condition is flawed; your shadowy and compulsion-ridden nature virtually ensures that you will hurt and be hurt. Without the marvelous peace-recapturing mechanism of forgiveness, you are open to the disharmonious and antiquated human condition of "an eye for an eye and a tooth for a tooth," which ensures that fighting never ceases.

These are merely a few of the choices that you're making constantly without conscious awareness that you're doing so. Try to become as aware as you can of choices you're making like these eleven above, and try to determine whether these decisions you're making are helping or hindering you in your caregiving endeavor. Try to forgive yourself of any "wrongs" you may be inadvertently committing, and try to affirm yourself for all the good you're doing.

*Because I care, I strive to show courage "under fire."*

# Caregiving Principle Six

## Develop and Follow a Personal Care Plan

My clinical experience assisting caregivers over the years has confirmed that the most common and most damaging caregiving mistake is trying to do too much! In a desire to give their very best, caregivers over-step their limits of endurance, over-extend their abilities, over-tax their personal resources, and over-estimate their time, energy, and stamina. They emotionally stretch themselves too far—sometimes even to a breaking point. They simply over-give and consequently set themselves up for a fall—a caregiving "crash and burn" event that causes them to either explode onto others or implode into themselves. The personal damage in either case is serious.

There are many, many varieties of over-doing, but any way that you overdo pulls you farther away from your spiritual strengths, farther away from your center of peace, and pushes you closer toward your shadows and compulsions—"places" of angst, anger, and agitation. Many caregivers live in a perpetual cycle of over-doing followed by a burnout event of some kind. To combat this tiresome and terrible repetitive rut, some caregivers develop negative "coping strategies" that only compound the problem. When a caregiver over-does, she generally over-reacts. They can over-eat, over-drink, they can inadvertently cut themselves off from friends and family, they become caregiving hermits in their own home, they can develop a "bad" attitude of irritation and frustration, they become negative, sour, sad, and they make more mistakes. Over-burdened caregivers over-worry: they mentally begin to "shut down," and their life descends into a conundrum of "shoulds" and "oughts," their self-esteem drops, and they become humorless. They begin to wear down and lose their personal caregiving edge little by little—they become unhappy and increasingly ineffective.

The only solution to counteract this dangerous cycle is to develop a personal caregiving plan. The goal of the plan is two-fold: 1) to give the best care to your care receiver and 2) to provide the best support to you—the caregiver. Your plan is your road map to health in body, mind, and spirit.

## Components of Your Illness Care Plan

A caregiving plan needs "moving parts." Here are ten parts or tools that you can use to construct your caregiving plan. Consider each with care, with reference to your receiver's needs as well as you own needs. Use the items and questions under each "tool" to help you actually write as comprehensive a caregiving plan as you can.

### Knowledge

Gather as much information about your care partner's diagnosis and about caregiving as you can. Knowledge is power, and power is what you need...not to be heavy-handed, but because knowledge arms you with the security of knowing what's real so you don't fall into the insecurity of unknowing. You need knowledge in several areas to include:

- Self-knowledge that comes primarily from your work with your spiritual strengths, shadows, and compulsions in the *"Spiritual Strengths 7-Week Immersion Program."* (See www.spiritualstrengthshealing.com).

- Information about caregiving the foundation of which is contained in the ten principles in this book.

- Information about community resources that comes from community referral agencies, such as Disease-specific organization like the American Cancer Society, local hospitals and other medical facilities, some social service agencies, and the like.

### Relationship

Work on the relationship with your care receiver as though it was your primary purpose...because it is. Caregiving is primarily relationship building. Relationship is the Alpha and the Omega of quality *caregiving*. (See principle #4.) Ask yourself the following questions:

- What can I do to improve my relationship with my care receiver?

- What would most help me improve my relationship with my care receiver?

- Which personality "voice" (strength, shadow, or compulsion) am I using when I talk with my care receiver?

### Boundaries

Establish caregiving boundaries: what you can do and what you cannot (or will not) do. Boundaries are imperative for your health and for clear communication with your care receiver. Ask yourself the following questions:

- What are the limits of my capabilities?

- Which of my spiritual strengths can I employ to help me decide upon and communicate the boundaries that are most healthy for me?

- How do I "draw the line" with my illness care receiver?

## Help

You are not alone; there are many, many resources for help that you can access. The barrier to securing help is not in its availability, but in hurdling over your interior attitudinal barriers that constantly remind you that you're supposed to do it all alone.

- Am I somehow communicating to family, friends, etc. that I am the only one who can perform caregiving tasks?
- What shadow or compulsion might be inhibiting me from seeking help?
- How do I best ask for help?

## Communication

Become clear and direct in your communication (See next chapter for more details). Ask yourself the following questions:

- Do I speak to my care receiver in ways that are understandable?
- Am I more empathic or more directive with my care receiver?
- Do I speak to my care receiver as a child or as an adult?

## Perspective

Take a step back and gain objective perspective. So many times, caregivers can't see the forest through the trees; they are too close to their care receiver and this blurs their evaluation of what is necessary now. Consult chapters 7 and 8 in Discover Your Spiritual Strengths, and ask yourself the following questions:

- How can I see my caregiving differently? Do I need to?
- How are others seeing my caregiving activities?
- How can I change my insight about my role as a caregiver and my outlook about my care receiver?

*Self-Care*

Self-care includes many things, but perhaps the most flagrant violation of self-care that I see in caregivers is failing to give themselves adequate breaks. Take frequent and planned breaks. The old adage of leisure goes something like this, *"You must regularly vacate your routines to remain focused upon them."* Chapter 9 in my book, Creating a Successful Retirement has a thorough overview of the recuperative value of leisure and its importance for overall wellness and stamina. Ask yourself the following questions:

- What shadow or compulsion might be preventing me from taking better care of myself?

- What is my history with caring for myself?

- Does my sense of personal worthiness interfere with my self-care needs?

*Confidante*

Study after research study affirms that the number one factor that grants any individual a heightened sense of self-esteem and life satisfaction (happiness) is having another person who is your champion, your informal counselor, your supporter, and your friend; a person who loves you warts and all. Ask yourself the following questions:

- Who is my confidante, that person with whom I can share the events and feelings of my *caregiving* life...someone who can listen and give constructive comment without soliciting unwanted advice?

- Who will love me no matter what?

- Who will be with me tomorrow, not judge me, but just be with me, so I can go on and do it all over again?

## Schedule

A plan and a schedule are indispensable for quality caregiving. Regularity is a good thing; habituation is not. Regularity gives order and symmetry to your life and your work. A schedule takes away your need to plan minute-by-minute, which is so stress-producing and inefficient. Ask yourself the following questions:

- What is the "main thing" for my *caregiving* today; what are the absolute "musts" to which I need to attend?

- What are my priorities today? What needs to be done first, and second, and third, etc.?

- What tools do I need to make and keep my schedule?

## Personality

Always remember that your personality is your primary caregiving tool. Your spiritual strengths, the power of your personality, need nourishment and refreshment. Pray, spend time with the Lord, see your strengths all around you, devote each day to one of your strengths and see how uplifted and energized you become. Ask yourself the following questions:

- How can I stay focused on my spiritual needs during this caregiving time?

- How much energy am I expending unnecessarily? How much energy am I giving to tension and turmoil within me? How can I quench my thirsty shadows and compulsions so I can stay as centered in my "true" personality as possible?

- How can I punctuate my day with prayer so I can remember who I really am and maintain my connection with the divine?

*Because I care, I put together a caregiving plan.*

# Caregiving Principle Seven

## Learn and Practice the Art of Simple and Direct Communication

While your personality, graced by your unique spiritual strengths, is your most powerful caregiving tool, it's your language—the very words you use and the emotion behind them—that is the most effective conduit of healing that you are called to be as a caregiver. There is nothing that can replace a compassionate voice, a tender word, a genuine sentiment, or a thought offered in clarity to create an environment of healing. In a very real sense, your words represent who you are; your language portrays your heart and sets the standard of care as nothing else can.

Each of your spiritual strengths has its own voice; these voices convey the best of who you are. These are the most attractive, compelling, and healing voices you can use. These voices are gifts from God that contain a celestial resonance of love. Your job as a caregiver is to speak from these voices of strength as much as possible. This may seem like an alien concept—to speak with voices sounds a bit spooky—but in fact, you've always used various voices in different situations. You have an authoritative voice when you want to convince or direct; you have a tender voice when you want to convey heartfelt sentiment; you have an angry voice, a diligent voice, an obedient voice, a challenging voice, and so on. In your vocation as a caregiver, you want to use the voices that flow from your spiritual strengths because these voices speak from your spirit-center. These are the most genuine and effective voices you have. These voices will promote your caregiving goals most accurately and efficiently, and with the greatest impact.

Actors put much effort into adopting many different voices to develop a repertoire of communication styles and patterns—each conveying a new range of sentiment and nuance. They expand their acting abilities and develop more presence by voice variation. This is not a false or ingenuine technique designed to fool an audience, but a means to project a clearer, cleaner message on stage. You want to do the same. You want your communication to be clean, clear, crisp, and as direct as possible. This is why we seek to tap into our spiritual strengths as our source of communication power.

## *Facilitative Communication Skills*

This chapter covers some fundamental, necessary and sufficient caregiving communication skills. These skills are indeed important. The voice you use in expressing these skills makes all the difference in how you "come across" and how effective your words will be…the degree of impact these skills will have for you. The skills can be powerful, but only when they are animated with/by a genuine voice, a voice that originates in your core.

*Quality communication is the beating heart of a quality caregiving relationship.*

## *The Value of Listening*

Active listening means to understand the full meaning of what your care receiver is trying to communicate. Listening is much more than not talking…it involves putting your full energies into discerning the entire message being communicated—even the "sub-messages" that your care receiver is indirectly saying perhaps without his awareness. Genuine listening establishes trust that boosts self-esteem and creates the framework for a healing relationship. "Listening to heal" gives you a broader and deeper understanding of your care receiver; you come to know him better. This focused and deepening communication begins to generate a true connection. A new relationship condition emerges, framed and supported by unspoken understanding and honest honoring, that leaches out any potential emotional toxins that might pollute a growing healing environment. The relationship itself becomes a healing mechanism.

## The Value of Silence

Silence can create a contemplative atmosphere that can foster healing. Sometimes in your stressed state you may feel the compulsion to fill each and every moment with words. While words are powerful and additive, meaningless words can confuse and frustrate, and eat away at the depth of the encounter; they trivialize what otherwise might be profound. Silence truly is golden. A peaceful silence adds accent to what came before and what comes after. When given with a gentle smile, silence adds to healing and creates a sense of sacredness in communication that otherwise might simply be dry, factual exchange.

## Attending

Attending means to "be with" another person fully. When you are in the moment of the person, when you are genuinely present and focused on the "now," you are attending fully. There are three levels of attending:

### Physical Attending

Your body is a valuable communicator of attending. When you—

- Face your care receiver squarely, you are saying, *"I'm with you."*

- Adopt an open posture, you communicate ease and relaxation.

- Lean toward your care receiver ever so slightly, you give a sign of availability and presence.

- Maintain good eye contact, you show respect.

- Remain relatively relaxed, you're saying that, *"I am at home with you."*

### Psychological Attending

This means that you are alert to the non-verbal as well as the verbal messages in your care receiver's communications to you. You notice such things as: tone of voice, inflection, word spacing, facial expressions, emphasis, pauses, and what are called "para-linguistic" comments such as: *Uh huh, OK, hmmm, tisk,* and other verbal sounds and expressions that add color and new levels of meaning to the communication. Giving subtle encouragements to talk is perhaps the most facile way of eliciting more psychological "material."

### Spiritual Attending

Listening for the spiritual material in the message is vitally important in our context of spiritual strengths caregiving. The best way to do this is to become increasing aware of how your care receiver communicates *his* spiritual strengths. Some people express their strengths directly, but most do so by exposing their shadows and compulsions—either directly or indirectly. When you "catch" your care receiver expressing a shadow or compulsion of any kind or nature, try to flip the conversation to the spiritual strength that is underlying the shadow or compulsion. For example, if your care receiver talks of being disillusioned, dispirited, sad, or even irritable, chances are that these have something to do with despair...which is the shadow of hope. You can train yourself to pick up these subtle signals and shift the conversation back to the spiritual strength. In this case, you may want to respond with a statement that in some way mentions or makes reference to hope. Your care receiver will not see this as contradictory, but rather complementary and affirming.

## Connie and Her Husband

What follows is a dialogue that we will use as a case study. It is a conversation between Connie (the caregiver) and her husband ([Connie's] care receiver).

**Connie**: Good morning, Hun. How are you feeling today?

**Husband**: Oh, not too good today.

**Connie**: What's wrong?

**Husband**: I'm just so dragged out; I can't seem to get going.

**Connie**: Well, you know that you shouldn't spend so much time watching TV. If you got a little exercise, like the doctor suggests, you wouldn't feel so tired all the time.

**Husband**: Oh, what does he know?

**Connie**: Well, anyone can see that you need to get up and get around. You don't go anywhere, even though you could if you wanted to. You don't even invite people over to visit with you. Sometimes I think you don't want to get fully well again.

**Husband**: I just wish I could see you when you get sick like me.

**Connie**: Oh, you're just depressed because nobody seems to call you anymore.

**Husband**: Oh yes they do call. You're just never here when they do.

**Connie**: Hun, you know that's simply not true. I'm here almost all the time. I do know who calls and who doesn't. Are you taking the medications that your doctor has prescribed for your mood? I'll just bet you're not!

**Husband:** [Holding back anger] Connie, why are you so hard on me?

**Connie:** I'm not being hard; you just think I am because you're not doing what you know is right.

**Husband:** [Now very angry] I try, I really do, but you don't seem to care anymore.

**Connie:** [Trying to pacify] Now, now, Hun, it's all right. You're going to be just fine.

**Husband:** I don't know about that. It doesn't feel like you're in my corner anymore.

**Connie:** I am in your corner, and I'm sure you will get better. Just do what the doctor and I tell you. If you do that, you'll be fine.

As you can see, this conversation went nowhere. As you examine the conversation, you'll notice that Connie committed the three most common communication mistakes:

### Unsolicited Advice

When Connie said, "Well, you know that you shouldn't spend so much time watching TV; if you got a little exercise, like the doctor suggests, you wouldn't feel so tired all the time." she was giving unsolicited advice. Notice the "should" statement in this response. Even if these words were said in a benign and even caring way, they still have all sorts of negative overtones and create an emotional undertow for your care receiver.

### Analyzing & Interpretation

When Connie said, "Oh, you're just depressed because nobody seems to call you anymore." and "Sometimes I think you don't want to get fully well again." She was actually analyzing and interpreting. Such statements are inherently disrespectful even if they are not meant to be.

### False Reassurance

When Connie said, *"Now, now, Hun, it's all right; you're going to be just fine,"* she was giving false reassurance. There is a place for genuine assurance, which offers hope and support; but giving false reassurance gives the opposite message. When not all facts are known, false assurance gives a hollow, insincere message that is simply not genuine. False reassurance indirectly tells your care receiver that you're not dealing with reality—you are simply placating your care receiver...who will eventually react negatively in some way.

Now, let's look at what Connie might have done to prevent the nightmare interchange that took place.

*Non-judgmental communication means learning to suspend your own evaluation in deference to your care receiver's opinions and preferences.*

### Stop Any Criticism

Give up your attitudinal "shoulds and "oughts" for your care receiver because they only get interpreted into statements that seem like criticisms. Criticism is the very opposite of helping behavior. Criticism communicates superiority, haughtiness, and cheerlessness. All these invade the emerging healing relationship that is the "holy grail" of facilitative communication.

### Exploration

Exploration means identifying the "facts" that are relevant in the communication; what exactly is your care receiver trying to say? What is the fullest and most accurate meaning of this communication? Beyond active listening and attending, Connie needed to do some exploring. What was the exact meaning of her husband's words? What was he trying to say when he said, "*Oh, not (feeling) too good today.*" What was the emotion under the statement? Connie needed to be sensitive to the emotional underpinnings of what her husband was saying.

### Concreteness

Concreteness means trying to sort through the communication and discover the most salient, important parts of what's being said. To be concrete means to help your care receiver be precise, accurate, and fully on-target with their meaning. Concreteness is achieved by asking questions in a patient and interested manner. When Connie's husband said, "*Oh, what does he know?*" referring to his doctor, was he expressing difficulty in following his instructions? Might his statement have been an expression of anger at his physician—or maybe at himself?

### Accurate Empathy

Empathy means that you look for the feelings and emotions that motivate your care receiver to say what they're saying. Words covey meaning, yet motivating feelings always undergird the meaning of the words. Empathy means that you focus on these underlying emotions of great merit. More than simply identifying the feelings that motivate words and word choice, empathy requires you to formulate a response that uses the feelings word that best describes the emotion under the factual statement. This process is known as "reflection of feelings." You become like a mirror reflecting back the underlying motivational feelings that go unsaid by your care receiver but which are rich with meaning. When you talk, you are always seeking to convey the fullest meaning you can. You can be maximally helpful to your care receiver when you take the extra step of discerning feelings and mirroring them back. When Connie's husband said, "*I try, I really do, but you don't seem to care anymore,*" what were the feelings underneath his statement?  Was he feeling: dejected, downcast, dismal, sorrowful, or gloomy?  Could Connie's husband be feeling flustered, confused, trapped, shattered, powerless, or simply exhausted?  Whatever his feelings, Connie needed to be more attentive to the full and complete message—including the emotional foundation that motivated the statement in the first place.

## Review

Here's a succinct sequence of basic communication skills.  This can serve as a review that you can consult from time to time to realign your thinking and readjust how you're using the language of *caregiving*.

- Active listening.
- Attending behaviors.
- Clarify meaning, be concrete.  Examples include:
  a. *"You mean…"*
  b. *"Do I hear you saying…?"*
  c. *"Could I check this out…"*
  d. *"Help me understand.  You're saying…"*
- Identify the motivating feelings.  Examples include:
  a. *"You feel…"*
  b. *"So you're feeling…"*
  c. *"It must be difficult for you to feel so…"*
  d. *"How do you feel about that?"*
- Give an affirming and understanding reason for the feeling.  Examples include:

a. *"You feel _____ because*

_____.*"*

b. *"I wonder if you're feeling*

_____ *because*

_____?*"*

c. *"Could it be that you feel*

_____ *because*

_____?*"*

d. *"Your feeling of*

_____ *is*

*understandable to me since*

_____.*"*

---

*Because I care, I regard my care receiver's feelings as important.*

# Caregiving Principle Eight

## Caregiving is Your Master Teacher

Every stage and phase of life offers its unique learning pearls. From infancy to elderhood, you walk through successive learning sequences that enhance you and bring you closer to the special "true self,"—that unique child of God who is genuinely you. Caregiving has a curriculum of life learning all its own. It offers you an in-depth study of human and faith development that you couldn't find anywhere else.

Certainly you learn about sickness, its impact, physiology, treatment, and biology. Yet, this is not the most challenging nor the most transformative learning you can receive as a caregiver. Far more poignant than learning about the illness of sickness is what you learn about the many touch points between the material manifestation of illness (the sickness of illness) and its emotional, psychological, and spiritual impacts on the human condition (the illness of sickness). Caregiving is truly a crash course in learning the deeper meaning of life itself.

### Find the Awe, Wonder & Delight in Caregiving

While it sounds contradictory, caregiving offers a vitalizing curriculum of joy that is yours to appreciate...or overlook. A very common caregiver lament is, "*I feel so stressed!*" Stress is the personality-contorting consequence of being either over- or under-stimulated. Caregivers generally are the former. Yet, joy is the opposite of stress. Caregiver stress comes from feeling insecure, feeling a sense of foreboding about the future, feeling overwhelmed by so much to do, yet not knowing where to start or how to proceed. Stress comes from feeling unprepared and "clueless" about having so few tools to accomplish the daunting tasks at hand.

Joy isn't about "having fun" as much as it's about being aware of what's real.

Awe, wonder, and delight help you suspend your stress. You find that you have fewer "shoulds" and "oughts" to clog-up your personality and inhibit your spiritual strengths. You learn to suspend judgment and overcome criticism (generally self-criticism). You feel joy, not as a "heel-clicking," "isn't this all wonderful" feeling, but rather as a still, clear, and solid feeling that God is in charge and you don't have to be. You suspend any fault-seeking and engage in joy-finding. Joy isn't about "having fun" as much as it's about being aware of what's real. To find this joy requires that you shift your attitudes about illness and caregiving from "ego attitudes" that stifle you to "Whole Self" attitudes that set you free.

## Damaging Caregiving Attitudes

### Damaging Attitude #1: I need my care receiver's approval.

Everyone wants to be liked, and without realizing it, we enter into approval-seeking behaviors. Caregivers can be particularly susceptible to this horrid attitude because we feel so sorry for our care receiver. We generally enter into endless attempts to gain approval from our care receiver, even when we're not at all aware that we're doing it. We can give out unconscious "messages" that we're not worthy. We emotionally discount ourselves and enter into self-blame. We need to shift our attitude to something more elevating, more accurate, and more constructive.

*Enriching Attitude:*
*I am complete just the way I am.*
*There is no lack within me.*

**Damaging Attitude #2: I feel so guilty most of the time.**

Guilt is so common among illness caregivers that it can almost seem universal. We think that we're not enough, that our care receiver needs more of us, and that we're under-performing. Attitudes like these rob us of our motivation that is so necessary. Guilt is a very ineffective motivator; it demeans us, clouds our vision, and leads to very low energy. We need to shift this attitude to something like...

*Enriching Attitude:*
*I can achieve inner peace through forgiveness.*

**Damaging Attitude #3: I need peace at any price.**

Disagreement is a part of any human relationship, and it certainly is a very common part of caregiving. You can't avoid disagreement...you can't possibly control both your personality and your care receiver's personality. Peace at any price really means that you are setting yourself up for a dishonest relationship with your care receiver, one that lacks clarity, candor, and forthrightness. Such a relationship is not healing for your *care receiver* because it isn't real; it makes no allowance for the intimacy of genuineness.

*Enriching Attitude:*
*Disagreement is normal and useful in any*
*caregiving relationship.*

**Damaging Attitude #4: I'm the victim of this caregiving situation; I'm always in the middle trying to do too much.**

When you see yourself as a victim, you naturally feel helpless and certainly unhappy. The caregiving role is not a prison; you are not a hostage to it. Thoughts like this damage your peace of mind and sabotage your countenance. You can substitute the word "learner" for the word "victim" to counteract tendencies like this damaging attitude. Learners carry much lighter burdens than do victims.

*Enriching Attitude:*
*I am a learner and not a victim in my caregiving role.*

**Damaging Attitude #5: If I'm not super-responsible, then I'm not worthy.**

Caregivers want to measure up to the task; they want to be seen as successful—especially if they feel the pressure that others (siblings, adult children, friends, etc.) are watching them. Such an attitude can generate some perfectionistic standards that will eventually swallow you up.

*Enriching Attitude:*
*I am worthy simply because of who I am and not because of what I do.*

**Damaging Attitude #6: I feel so sorry for my care receiver.**

Feeling sorry is all about you and not about your care receiver. While feeling sorry is a natural reaction, it's less than optimal in the caregiving situation for two reasons: 1) It communicates a level of insincerity to your care receiver, and 2) It uses up lots of emotional energy in you that could be better spent on more constructive emotional responses, or simply conserved as a rest for you.

*Enriching Attitude:*
*I have faith that there is a reason for illness; in some mysterious way it is part of God's plan.*

**Damaging Attitude #7: Only I can help my care receiver.**

This again is a common, although most times unrealized attitude that many illness caregivers adopt. The attitude of "specialness," that you are somehow the only one who can offer caregiving is not only false, it's also somewhat selfish. You may be your care receiver's spouse and therefore feel that all caregiving is your responsibility, and yet even in this very close relationship, both you and your care receiver need a break from one another. There are many reasons why you might feel this responsibility or even a sense of entitlement—all of which rest in your attitudes about you, your needs, and your best interests. The antidote for such a situation is to consult your spiritual strengths; to enlist their divine support. Ask the Holy Spirit for help in discerning why you might feel so responsible and how you might be able to move beyond it.

*Enriching Attitude:*
*I'm part of a caregiving team that wants the very best for my care receiver.*

**Damaging Attitude #8:  I can't stand to see my care receiver angry or resentful, she needs to be calm and at peace.**

The caregiving situation is fraught with emotions of all kinds that all clash and bash together and sometimes create emotional earthquakes in the everyday relationship between you and your care receiver. Emotional turmoil is not only common; it may actually be beneficial when it brings about a realignment or review of the relationship that may need readjustment. Let the emotions you encounter in yourself and in your caregiving relationship just "be." You needn't protect yourself or your care receiver from what you might consider the sharpness of emotions. Within limits, even sharp emotions—when heard with the ears of your spirituals strengths—clear the air and bring refreshment to a parched caregiving earth.

*Enriching Attitude:*
*My care receiver is the way she has always been,*
*but the illness is making it more so.*

**Damaging Attitude #9: I can fix, or should be able to find a solution for, any of my care receiver's problems.**

Just because you are the primary caregiver does not automatically give you super-human abilities to achieve anything and everything. Your care receiver's "problems" are many times unfixable; they have no solution on the material plane. The only "solution" to all things is an internal or "elegant" solution where you shift your personality: you change some of your beliefs, your perceptions, your thinking, your feelings, your decisions, and your actions...you engage your spiritual strengths.

*Enriching Attitude:*
*Only things can be fixed; people are healed,*
*but only if they want to be.*

**Damaging Attitude #10: I can (should) do it all.**

Being all things to all people is, of course, quite impossible. Yet, so many caregivers stumble over this most obvious truth. They illogically believe that because they have been given the job of the primary caregiver that miraculously they should have the time, energy, expertise, understanding, and stamina to "do it all." The fallacy of this idea is apparent to all, even those caregivers who violate it the most. Somehow we have the erroneous idea that these "illogical truths" pertain to other people but not to us. It's hard to embrace even our most illogical, shadowy and compulsive-ridden thinking as our own; nonetheless, this is perhaps the biggest challenge of caregiving.

*Enriching Attitude:*
*Today I choose only peace,*
*not necessarily productivity.*

The wording of these attitudes may not "fit" your particular caregiving situation. Re-work them so that they are more accurate for you...try to "hear what they're trying to tell you." Try to see where they are pointing.

*Because I care, I seek to be a harmonizing*
*influence.*

# Caregiving Principle Nine

## Creative Acceptance—Letting-Go is Your Most Valuable Promoter of Peace of Mind and Heart

Some years ago, I had the pleasure of counseling a woman who was caring for her father who suffered with advanced prostate cancer. One day, she lamented in our session that she now realized what she called the "craziness" of approaching her caregiving responsibilities in exactly the same way as she always had. She related that she was making the same mistakes over and over again. She didn't exactly know what the mistakes were, but her new revelation made it imperative that she shift her caregiving gears.

She explained that she needed to look at her father and her caregiving role with "new eyes." This was not a denial of reality, she reasoned, but instead a means of perceiving reality more clearly and more accurately than she had been—to be more accepting of what was true. She wanted to do things in a different way, adopt a new sense of what she termed "yielding," because the way she was running her life was simply not working. What she related seemed to be giving greater definition—and certainly practical meaning—to a whole new notion, one I have come to call "creative acceptance."

Frustration and irritation, guilt and remorse are all too common emotional intruders in the caregiving experience. When you feel low, sad, blue, discouraged, disillusioned, etc., realize that these are but affective nudges...reminders that something needs to change. Perhaps you need to make some changes in your caregiving efforts; chances are that these changes need to take place within you. You're called at such times to view what you're doing through "new eyes." Your view of reality may be causing you emotional pain—pushing you away from rather than toward—your care receiver. Perhaps you need a new attitude and perhaps even a new vision so you can become more accepting of what is true.

## Creative Acceptance

Change comes in many forms. One avenue of change is moving to creative acceptance. I use the word "creative" to distinguish this type of acceptance, which is strong and has no hint of submission or resignation, from "mere" acceptance that is weak and hints at fearful retreat. Creative acceptance aligns more with words like detachment, intentional surrender, distancing, disengagement, letting things "be," and simply letting-go. Creative acceptance is not "giving-up," "throwing in the towel," or "running away." Rather, creative acceptance involves a rugged "taking on." It is purposeful strength and steadfast presence, it is determination, "true grit," and courageous risk. It's all of these things and one more...and it's necessary for successful caregiving!

Creative acceptance is essentially spiritual. It brings you to another realm, a realm of the spirit where you're called to exercise faith so you can transcend a simple worldly reality and take on a more cosmic one. Creative acceptance requires prayer so you can meet the mystery of the next plane and build a bridge from caregiving anxiety to creative caregiving peace. Creative acceptance is a triumph not a defeat; it is a transformative challenge, a wake-up call to take a non-resistant stance in harmony and personality integrity. You eventually let-go of any need to control, you let-go of predetermined expectations and desired consequences...you let-go of your will and take on God's will. This is no small order.

*Control begets illness and loss of self, whereas acceptance fosters health and self-preservation.*

Creative acceptance requires a live-in-the-present attitude, which builds hope and drowns out despair. Acceptance begets inner peace, a calm of heaven right here and right now. It is comforting and affirming, trusting and loving. Creative acceptance transforms your perceptual focus by moving it away from what you are losing and shifting it to what you are gaining: an abundance of spirit. Creative acceptance allows you to see caregiving as a learning process of addition, not a diminishment process leading only to attrition. Creative acceptance is not a state of being; rather, creative acceptance is a process of becoming...becoming closer to God by using the healing graces inside you. Acceptance is an ideal; you can never completely achieve it, but you can grow closer and closer to it. You are not called to attain perfect acceptance. You are merely called to accept it as your goal!

Perhaps illness is not the cause of all your problems; perhaps the way you look at illness is your culprit. Creative acceptance calls you to re-forge the tool of your personality, like turning your swords into plowshares, so you can stop destroying and begin planting seeds for new growth. Acceptance may be your number one caregiving need. What else but acceptance can pull you out of the quicksand of all your negative emotions and allow you to stand on firm ground where you can trust and once again feel secure.

There is a paradox here, a paradox similar to the first step of the Alcoholics Anonymous (AA) Program, which states that, "I am powerless over alcohol." Logic alone might lead you to think that if you are powerless over alcohol that you could not stop yourself from drinking more. Paradoxically, the opposite is true; when you *admit* your powerlessness, you in some mysterious way gain more power...or perhaps you can now access the power that already exists within you in your spiritual strengths. In the same way, acceptance paradoxically gives you more power—allowing you to tap into the power source within you and find new peace, understanding, and compassion. Acceptance electrifies your energies, allowing you to be much more than you otherwise thought possible.

> *Powerlessness is not helplessness, and creative acceptance is not resignation. Both offer peace beyond our human understanding.*

### First Seek Peace

Not long after I began working with caregivers, when I was actively facilitating many caregiver support groups, I realized that I could divide all caregivers into two categories or groups. The first group required a much greater need to control their caregiving role in general and their care receivers in particular. Folks in this first group claimed that they either had control or they were actively working to achieve control. The second group of folks registered no such control needs. Not surprisingly, the first group reported higher levels of anger with themselves and their care receivers. Furthermore, they registered levels of guilt commensurate with their higher levels of anger. The second group reported feeling neither anger nor guilt.

The coping strategies used by the two groups were decidedly different as well. The first group seemed to desire an ever-increasing need to "get on top of the situation," and to find solutions to problems presented by the caregiving situation. By contrast, members of the second group were much more inclined to accept the condition of their care receiver and its consequences in ways that were non-controlling. My observation indicated that the members of the first group were inclined to resist the situation of their care receiver, while the second group seemed to "flow" with it. This latter approach to caregiving is one of creative acceptance. They registered little if any resistance to reality and displayed very little criticism or even judging behaviors. Not surprisingly, members of this second group were happier and more at peace.

## *How to "Let Go"*

The World Federation of Alcohol Abuse has developed a fascinating definition of "letting-go" that I think has clear application here in the caregiving setting. Ponder the meaning of these items as they relate to your *caregiving* situation:

To let-go—

- Does not mean to stop caring; it means I can't do it for someone else.

- Is not to cut myself off; it is the realization that I cannot control another or the situation.

- Is not to enable, but to allow learning from natural consequences.

- Is to admit powerlessness, which means the outcome is not in my hands.

- Is not to try to change or to blame another, but to make the most of myself.

- Is not to take care of so much as to care for and to care about.

- Is not to "fix," but to be supportive.
- Is not to judge, but to allow another to be a human being—to be perfectly imperfect.
- Is not to be in the middle, arranging all the outcomes, but to allow others to affect their own destinies.
- Is not to be protective, but to permit another to face reality.
- Is not to deny, but to move toward creative acceptance.
- Is not to nag, scold, or argue, but to search out my own shortcomings and correct them.
- Is not to adjust everything to my desires, but to take each day as it comes and to cherish myself as God's child.
- Is not to criticize and regulate anybody, but to try to become what I dream I can be.
- Is not to regret the past, but to appreciate the present and grow and live for the future.
- Is to fear less and love more.

Every one of these may not apply directly to your caregiving situation. Pick about three of these definitions that "ring true" in your caregiving journey and begin to apply them. Ask yourself what needs to be done to move this caregiving notion into your illness care.

*Because I care, I seek to bring an inspiring heart to my care receiver.*

# Caregiving Principle Ten

## Act with Confidence: You are Never Alone in Your Caregiving; God is Always with You.

Caregiving brings you into intimate contact with life itself. As you look deeply into the eyes of your care receiver, realize that you are encountering not only the core of that person, but you are also encountering yourself. When you look deeply enough you can sense the connectedness of all life, which leads you to the power of divinity...the healing power of God. Caregiving brings you in contact with God in ways that you could not otherwise experience. Caregiving is a privilege, indeed a revered and exalted role of honor where you can everywhere catch glimpses of God flashing like reminders of goodness and light. You are on holy ground, and you must tread lightly and reverently.

### *Special Caregiving Grace*

As I survey the incredible stamina, perseverance, and courage of illness caregivers, I come to the conclusion that caregivers do indeed receive special grace. This renewing and refreshing power and might from God provides you with new eyes and invigorated hands to "see" clearer and to "do" with renewed confidence. It is grace that pulls you through situations that you thought you could never accomplish yourself; indeed you cannot do this on your own and it's almost inhuman to expect that you can. You can only do it with God's help...with God's special caregiving grace.

Become ever more aware of this grace, come to expect it with hope and not presumption, and come to depend on it as a holy presence that makes all thing new.

### Become Aware That Your Caregiving is Part of the Abundance

It's easy to lapse into lamentation with thoughts like, *"Why does there have to be illness?" "Why does God allow this to happen?" "Illness is destroying all that I hold dear."* Such thinking, while somewhat logical on a very simplistic level, is nonetheless irrelevant and even delusional when you come to see that illness is part of the mystery of life that paradoxically brings you closer to life and love, not farther away from it. Certainly there must be a purpose of all of this, but when viewed through your human eyes only, when you take only a worldly view of illness, it pulls you into believing that all of this is a senseless and tortuous descent into oblivion. Such thinking diminishes you, it contorts you. It is shadow and compulsion thinking and not spiritual strengths thinking. Such thinking can only bring you down.

*Illness challenges you to remember that God uses your natural human condition as marvelous instruction for you to better learn the power of love.*

When viewed through the eyes of God, illness becomes a vehicle for learning your true reality as a child of God. You come to better understand that there is no contradiction of God's promise of abundance. Illness teaches you to see life in an entirely different, spiritual light.

## Elsie

Several years ago, I encountered a person with Parkinson's Disease who changed the way I viewed illness and *caregiving* forever. Elsie was 72 when I first began counseling with her. Over more than several sessions, she related to me that she had always suffered from depression. She had sought professional help since she was a very young woman and this continued even till this day. Indeed, Elsie had been hospitalized for depression three times in her life. In many ways she had a tough life, yet there was within her a surprising stamina, a rock-like quality deep inside that had given her direction and purpose through her years. Now that she was diagnosed with Parkinson's, this special quality, this amalgam of spiritual strength, seemed to become ever more evident in her personality.

It was during one of our counseling sessions that she said something that I shall never forget. She said, *"I'm glad I have Parkinson's because now people know that I'm really sick."* I was thrown back in my chair by this statement. Instead of seeing it as a manipulative means of drawing more sympathy from others, or as a way of becoming even more dependent than she had been, I saw this statement as testimony of her internal strength. At last she could be taken seriously, at last people would know that she does indeed suffer; people understood...her external, physical symptoms were evident. People understand Parkinson's so much more than they can understand long-standing depression.

From that day, Elsie's mood shifted. She emotionally rallied, her thinking became so much clearer; her feelings lifted, and she could make decisions without the internal turmoil that had previously characterized her choices. For all intents and purposes, Elsie became a new person. I had occasion to visit with her adult children who reported that, in their words, *"Our mother is back,"* and *"I'm now talking to an adult again, she had been so child-like for so many years."* Elsie lived three more years, and all who knew her reveled in her newfound personal confidence and internal harmony.

Elsie had a deep faith.  Through all the years of depression, even though Elsie felt quite alienated from others at times, she had a friend in God.  Her faith in God carried her; God was indeed her companion through it all.  Now, in this new crisis, Elsie was truly blessed because not only was God with her, but God had brought new understanding into the hearts and minds of those people who Elsie loved, and who, despite all her alternating desperate and sometimes angry depression, always loved her too.  Now they could express their love clearer; now they could demonstrate their love openly and freely.  Elsie's sickness brought her to a new beginning of her life; it gave her an entirely new perspective on life, on love, and on herself.

### Learn to Use Your Spiritual Strengths

God's special caregiver grace is nowhere better seen than in your spiritual strengths.  Here is the presence of the Almighty in you.  Few experiences teach you to apply your spiritual strengths better than caregiving. In what classroom could you better learn patience, acceptance, compassion, self-discipline, hope, wisdom, courage, and all the healing graces God makes available to you but in the *caregiving* arena?  The curriculum of caregiving is learning the magnificence and the power of your own healing graces, your own spiritual strengths.

The many losses that you confront in the face of caregiving are graces that point to your true and higher reality.  Deep inside of you rests your true essential self, your true essence.  Here throbs God's power in the form of the strengths given to you to use well.  The caregiving arena is one of the finest places to use these healing graces well.  Caregiving does ask you, indeed it requires you, to leave so much behind, to let-go of so much of what you formerly took for granted.

Illness pushes you to rearrange your attitudes about what's most important; it offers a new vision of life quite different, if not contradictory, from what you formerly perceived. It reshapes your thinking to conform to another reality beyond this world; it elevates your feelings beyond this plane and focuses them on another; it gives you choices of using your personality in ways you never thought possible; and it provides a stage upon which you can perform your life's work as never before. Indeed the gifts of caregiving are legion.

God's presence becomes ever so much more real through caregiving. As you go about your caregiving tasks, imagine that you are being followed by a holy presence, a benevolent enhancer of you, a gracious life-enricher who whispers encouragement, direction, and care into every fiber of your being. This presence is always there in you. When you recognize the presence and smile, even if you force a smile to remind you of the presence, your spiritual strengths are activated, your attitude lifts, your vision clears, your thinking elevates, your feelings shift to the positive, your choices are obvious, and your behaviors become love in action. You have entered the realm of newness, the abundance of grace, and the promise of eternal love.

# Appendix

## Assumptions of the Spiritual Strengths Healing Plan

Healing is best understood to proceed along all three levels of human experience: 1) body, 2) mind, and 3) spirit. **Maximal healing is achieved holistically**, i.e., each of these three levels of human experience must be addressed as a part of a larger unit...as part of a whole, which is more than the three parts taken individually.

The "mind" portion of the holistic perspective of healing is seen in the Spiritual Strengths Healing Plan as the **six operational functions of the personality**: 1) believing, 2) perceiving, 3) thinking, 4) feeling, 5) deciding, and 6) acting.

The "Spirit" portion of the holistic perspective is seen in the Spiritual Strengths Healing Plan as the special or **premier spiritual strength** (virtue) you have received in each of the six functions of your personality. You have been given one premier gift in each of the six functions for a total of six spiritual strengths...your special healing type...your spiritual fingerprint.

**Love** is the fundamental healing power; all energy flows from this central font of the power of Love. Love comes from God; it cannot be manufactured or synthesized by humans.

**Healing** is clearly distinguished from the medical concept of **curing**. Curing means restoring physical brokenness or malfunctioning **(sickness)** to a state of functionality. Healing, on the other hand, is seen as closing the gap in mind and/or spirit that was opened by your reactions to your sickness. This gap, usually expressed through personality pain, is what is called **illness**.

The more completely you can **open-up** to the healing power of God within you, the more you will benefit from these gifts of grace.

You have been endowed with spiritual strengths that are **particular, singular, specific, and unique** to you.

These personal spiritual strengths serve as your **primary means of achieving healing** and personal spiritual growth.

As you become increasingly **aware of your spiritual strengths**, you will quite naturally begin the process of folding the power of your spiritual strengths into your everyday life.

Each of your spiritual strengths has a corresponding **shadow**, a condition where the spiritual strength is absent. This shadow presents a special vulnerability or possible point of internal tension in you.

Likewise, each of your spiritual strengths has a corresponding **compulsion**, a condition where your ego has distended the strength to a point of distortion. This compulsion becomes a proclivity in you to move away from your spiritual strength and consequently away from your Real Self.

When shadows are brought to light, and compulsions are revealed as personality "terrorists", healing work quite naturally commences on the task of using your shadows and/or compulsions **in service of your healing** and enhanced spiritual growth.

The Spiritual Strengths Healing Plan is **not "faith healing"** where you rely on your internal mechanisms as the sole means for physical cure. **The Spiritual Strengths Healing Plan never promises cure**; its purpose is healing. The Method can however be seen as a supplement and support for traditional medical practices.  The philosophy of the Spiritual Strengths Healing Plan is that you should seek the best and most appropriate medical and psychological care you can in accord with your own personal wishes.

# End Note

To help you achieve such a dramatic re-sourcing of your personality that this book suggests, may I recommend that you consult the book: <u>The Ten Most Effective Self-Care Techniques: What You Can Do to Maximize Your Healing Journey</u>, which is another book in the Spiritual Strengths Healing Plan series. Pay special attention to the techniques of relaxation, meditation, and healing prayer. There you'll find specific ways you can discover new ways to communicate with the divine and become more receptive to the special illness caregiver grace that is everywhere.

May you discover the newness, the consistency, the wholeness, and the abundance of life through your illness care.

We are all blessed,

*Richard P. Johnson, Ph.D.*

Made in the USA
Middletown, DE
29 April 2015